A Tribute to
THE YOUNG AT HEART

LOUISA MAY ALCOTT

By Jill C. Wheeler

Published by Abdo & Daughters, 4940 Viking Drive, Suite 622, Edina, Minnesota 55435.

Raintree   1-12-96   13.99

Copyright © 1996 by Abdo Consulting Group, Inc., Pentagon Tower, P.O. Box 36036, Minneapolis, Minnesota 55435 USA. International copyrights reserved in all countries. No part of this book may be reproduced in any form without written permission from the publisher.

Printed in the United States.

Cover Photo credit: Archive Photos
Interior Photo credits: Archive Photos, pages 5, 10, 15, 23, 29, 31
Wide World Photos, page 7

Edited by Julie Berg

Library of Congress Cataloging-in-Publication Data

Wheeler, Jill C., 1964
        Louisa May Alcott / Jill C. Wheeler ; [edited by Julie Berg].
        p. cm. — (Young at heart)
Summary: A biography of the well known nineteenth-century American author whose popular novels, "Little Women" and "Little Men," were based on her own family experiences.
ISBN 1-56239-518-1
1. Alcott, Louisa May, 1832-1888—Biography—Juvenile literature. 2. Women authors, American—19th century—Biography—Juvenile literature.   [1. Alcott, Louisa May, 1832-1888. 2. Authors, American. 3. Women—Biography.] I. Berg, Julie. II. Title. III . Series Tribute to the young at heart.
PS1018.W48   1995
813'.4—dc20
[b]   95-4657
                                                                                                    CIP
                                                                                                    AC

TABLE OF CONTENTS

LITTLE WOMEN, BIG IDEAS

On Christmas Day 1994, moviegoers flocked to see a new release. It was the story of the four March sisters. They lived during the Civil War. The movie was *Little Women.*

Many people left the theater wiping tears from their eyes. The story they'd just seen moved them. The sisters—Meg, Jo, Beth and Amy—lived through many tough times. Love kept them together. Hope gave them strength.

The movie was based on a book written more than 100 years ago. The book also was called *Little Women.* Louisa May Alcott wrote the book. She told people she based it on her life. She said, "I am Jo."

Some people thought Louisa's life had been just like Jo's. Although similar, Louisa's life was even more colorful. She grew up on a commune. She was the first woman in her city to vote. She wrote blood-filled thrillers and tender, sweet stories. She worked as a nurse during the Civil War.

Louisa was ahead of her time in many ways. She died in 1888, yet her legacy lives on. People around the world read her books and stories to this day.

The 1994 Christmas hit movie *Little Women* starring Susan Sarandon and Wynona Rider. The movie was based on the Louisa May Alcott novel by the same title.

MOVING FROM TOWN TO TOWN

Louisa May Alcott was born November 29, 1832, in Germantown, Pennsylvania. Like Jo in *Little Women*, Louisa was one of four daughters. Her parents were Bronson and Abigail Alcott. The family called Abigail "Abba." Louisa called her "Marmee."

Louisa's family moved to Germantown so her father could run a special school. Bronson called the school "Pine Place." He had special ideas about teaching children. He believed learning should be fun. He made sure the lessons at Pine Place were entertaining. His school thrived for a short time.

Although Bronson had many ideas, he didn't have much money. Pine Place closed in March 1833. Without money from the school, the Alcotts had to move.

This was the first of many moves for Louisa. Her family moved twenty-nine times before she was twenty-eight years old.

The Old Bridge at Concord, Massachusetts, one of the many towns
in which Alcott lived as she grew up.

After Germantown, they moved to Philadelphia, then Boston where Bronson started another school.

Louisa enjoyed Boston. She had many adventures. Some of those stayed with her all her life. Once, she fell into a pond. A young African-American boy rescued her. She never forgot his help.

As she grew, Louisa learned about slavery. Louisa hated the idea of slavery. She believed people should treat everyone the same. So did her father. He invited an African-American girl to study at his school. Many of the parents of Bronson's other students disagreed with him. They pulled their children out of his school. Once again, his school failed and the family had to move. This time they chose Concord, Massachusetts.

TOMBOY SCHOLAR

Bronson's friend, Ralph Waldo Emerson, had told the Alcotts about Concord. Louisa agreed that it was a wonderful place. She loved her days there. Their house was near a river, gardens and a big barn. There was plenty of room to play. In between playing, they studied.

Bronson and Abba felt education was very important, and taught their daughters well. Louisa liked most of her lessons. "I never liked arithmetic nor grammar, and dodged those branches on all occasions," she wrote later. "But reading, writing, composition, history, and geography I enjoyed, as well as the stories read to us."

One of Louisa's favorite books was *Pilgrim's Progress*. That book was a favorite of the March sisters, too. Like Jo, Louisa also was a tomboy. "I always thought I must have been a deer or a horse in some former state," she wrote. "It was such a joy to run. No boy could be my friend till I had beaten him in a race. No girl if she refused to climb trees, leap fences and be a tomboy."

The American author, Ralph Waldo Emerson, was a close friend of Louisa May Alcott's father, Bronson.

Louisa got into trouble often. She loved to take dares. Once she rubbed red pepper into her eyes. Another time someone dared her to jump off the roof of a barn. She did and sprained both ankles.

Though Louisa enjoyed Concord, her family's life was hard there. Bronson did not make much money. He could barely feed his family. Sometimes he gave away what little they had to poorer families. Louisa later described her family as "poor as rats."

When Louisa was nineteen, Bronson took a trip to England. He met people who talked about a new kind of life. Bronson liked their ideas. He decided to try them. The family moved again. They started a commune.

LIFE ON A COMMUNE

A commune is a place where everyone shares everything. Bronson thought this life would lead to peace and happiness. His friend, Ralph Waldo Emerson, agreed.

The Alcotts began their commune with three other men and a boy. They started it on a farm near Harvard, Massachusetts. The farm had apple trees, so they called it "Fruitlands." Louisa loved it, although her suppers often were fruit and bread. She worked hard to help with the farm. She also wrote a journal and poems.

The commune had some rules that other people found strange. The commune rules would not allow members to have items made of cotton. Plantations that grew cotton used slaves. The commune members were against slavery. Members could not use silk or wool, either. They felt using silk took advantage of silkworms. Using wool took advantage of sheep.

Sadly for Bronson, his experiment failed. The other people in the commune wanted to send Abba and the Alcott girls away. Bronson would not let that happen. The others left the commune less than a year after they moved there. The Alcott family was alone again and penniless.

Abba's family helped the Alcotts find a new place to live. Later, Abba inherited some money. Now the Alcotts could buy a small home in Concord.

The new house came with a shed. Abba had the shed added to the house so Louisa could have her own room. She knew Louisa wanted a special place all her own. Now, Louisa had a room and a mission. She was going to make money for the family. When she was only twelve, she made and sold doll dresses. She did whatever she could to help.

Her sewing made money. Yet her true love was writing. She wrote plays that she and her sisters acted out in their barn. They also had their own post office and a newspaper. Many of these activities showed up later in Louisa's books.

Ralph Waldo Emerson fueled Louisa's love of literature. He let her borrow books from his library. He also knew she wanted to earn money for the family. When she was sixteen, he suggested she start a school. He sent his children to be her students. One of them was Louisa's special student. Her name was Ellen. Louisa wrote stories for Ellen.

Louisa made a little money with her school, but not enough. Her mother eventually decided to take a job. Abba felt she had no other choice. Her job was in Boston, so the family moved back there.

This is the home where the Alcott family lived in Concord, Massachusetts.

A PUBLISHED AUTHOR

In Boston, Louisa was more determined than ever to help her family. She sewed and taught school. She desperately wanted to escape her life of poverty. "I'll be rich and famous and happy before I die," she said. "See if I won't."

She also vowed to become a better person. When she was seventeen, she noted this in her journal: "My quick tongue is always getting me into trouble. My moodiness makes it hard to be cheerful when I think how poor we are, how much worry it is to live, and how many things I long to do I never can."

Louisa dreamt of writing plays. She had written many when she was younger. She still wrote plays, and even came close to having one produced. Unfortunately, it did not happen. About the same time, Bronson found one of the tales Louisa had written for Ellen Emerson. He sent it to a publisher. The publisher printed it. He paid Louisa $5 for the story.

Later, a publisher printed all the stories Louisa had written for Ellen. He called the volume, *Flower Fables*. He paid Louisa $32 for the whole book. To Louisa, it was a fortune.

The next year, the Alcotts moved to New Hampshire. Louisa was glad to be back in the country. She knew she couldn't stay if she wanted to earn more money. She had to move back to Boston. It was the only way she could support her family.

Alone in Boston, she again taught, wrote stories and sewed. "Sewing won't make my fortune," she wrote in her journal. "But I can plan my stories while I work, and then scribble them down on Sundays." She sent her money back to her family. Soon she was supporting them by herself.

GOOD-BYE TO TWO SISTERS

While the Alcotts lived in New Hampshire, Abba nursed a sick family. Louisa's sisters, Elizabeth and May, were ill. Elizabeth never got better. The family knew she could not survive another harsh New Hampshire winter. They decided to move back to Concord.

But Elizabeth did not recover. She died on March 14, 1858. The next month, Louisa's older sister, Anna, got engaged. Now there was just Louisa to help her parents and youngest sister, May. She had to fix up the family's new home in Concord. The house was called "Orchard House." Louisa called it "Apple Slump." It needed many repairs.

Louisa knew she had to pay for repairs. She moved back to Boston and got a job tutoring a young woman. She also kept on writing. She discovered newspapers were hungry for stories full of adventure and romance. Louisa called them "trash and rubbish."

She penned tales of murders, suicides, drugs, and passion. She wrote them under the name A.M. Barnard. They helped her pay the bills. She decided to write these stories until she could afford to write what she wanted.

"I feel as if I could write better now, more truly of things I have felt and therefore know," she said. "I hope I shall yet do my great book, for that seems to be my work, and I am growing up to it."

Write she did. Sometimes Louisa would write for fourteen hours at a time. She pressed down so hard with her pen that she paralyzed her thumb. She stopped only to eat what her parents brought her. They gave her apple cider, squash pie and gingerbread. What interested other young women did not appeal to Louisa. She did not want to get married. "I would rather be a free spinster and paddle my own canoe," she said.

Freedom was important to Louisa. It upset her that not everyone in America was free. Slavery was still a concern for many people. It led to the Civil War. Louisa wished she could fight for her country.

Instead, she decided to become a nurse at a military hospital. In December 1862, she packed her bags and left for Washington, D.C.

THE HORRORS OF WAR

Louisa was unprepared for what awaited her in Washington. The military hospital was an old hotel. Rats and cockroaches scuttled through the filthy rooms. Cold winter air seeped in through broken window panes.

Days after she arrived, a big battle took place. The hospital quickly filled with wounded soldiers. The men were covered with mud. Louisa found the smell almost unbearable. She admired the soldiers' bravery under such conditions. "There they were!" she wrote later. "Our brave boys, as the papers justly call them." She complimented them for their courage when their bodies were "riddled with shot and shell, so torn and shattered."

Louisa had many jobs at the hospital. She cleaned up the ragged, blood-soaked soldiers. She wrote letters for them. She held their hands as they suffered in silence. She helped feed them. She listened to their stories.

She heard stories of bravery. She heard about loved ones. She heard about tragedy. She wrote those stories in letters to her family. After she left the hospital, a publisher saw the letters. Louisa earned $40 for the resulting book, *Hospital Sketches*. She kept writing other stories, too. In 1863, she made nearly $600 from her writings. It was enough to pay for more repairs to Orchard House.

Louisa rarely spent money on herself. Her characters often spoke of fancy dresses. Louisa usually wore a plain black or dark brown dress. She piled her thick chestnut hair on her head. She often looked sad. People thought she was older than she was.

She kept a brown velvet pillow on the living room sofa. She called it her "mood pillow." Sometimes she stood it up. Sometimes she laid it down. It was a signal to her family. It told them whether or not she felt like talking. She even wrote her first novel, titled *Moods*. Now people paid attention to Louisa May Alcott.

SUCCESS AT LAST

After *Moods,* Louisa took a job as a young woman's traveling companion. They went to Europe. Louisa enjoyed it so much she stayed for a year. When she returned, her family's bills had piled up again. She had to write again.

Her publisher wanted a book for girls. Louisa usually wrote for adults. Still, she said she would try. She began to outline a book based on her own life. "Marmee, Anna and May all approve of my plan," she wrote in her journal. "So I plod away, though I don't enjoy this sort of thing. Our queer plays and experiences may prove interesting, though I doubt it." Louisa called her book *Little Women*. She sent the first chapters to her publisher. "The publisher thought it flat and so did I," Louisa wrote. "Neither hoped much for or from it." She finished it anyway in July 1868. She recorded the event in her journal. "Have finished *Little Women* and sent it off — 402 pages. Very tired, head full of pain from overwork, and heart heavy about Marmee, who is growing feeble."

Lousia May Alcott became a successful children's book author.

The story of *Little Women* now is history. The first edition of the book sold out almost immediately. Louisa's publisher asked for another volume. Louisa quickly wrote part II. Today, *Little Women* includes both parts.

Many of Louisa's fans wrote to her. They asked who the March girls would marry. This upset Louisa. "Girls write to ask who the little women marry, as if that was the only end and aim of a woman's life," Louisa wrote. "I won't marry Jo to Laurie to please anyone."

Louisa paid off all the family's debts after she sold part II of *Little Women*. Finally, the Alcott family was debt-free. "My dream is beginning to come true," she wrote. "If my head holds out I'll do all I once hoped to do."

A POISON INSIDE

Louisa didn't know if her head would hold out. She had caught typhoid pneumonia while a nurse. She had been sick ever since. She had headaches, dizziness, and leg pains. Sometimes she couldn't sleep. At first, no one knew why. Then they discovered she had been poisoned. The medicine the doctors gave her for the pneumonia had mercury in it. Mercury stays in the body. It slowly poisons people.

Doctors could not help Louisa. She went on as best she could. She finished another novel despite her poor health. She titled it *Old Fashioned Girl*. "I wrote it with my left hand in a sling, one foot up, head aching, and no voice," she said.

Readers loved *Old Fashioned Girl*. Louisa decided to celebrate her success. She went to Europe again. This time, she went with her sister May and one of May's friends. The three women spent a year in Europe. Louisa's publishers wrote to her. They asked for more stories. Louisa wrote back that she was on vacation. She sent them a silly poem instead.

Then Louisa learned that Anna's husband had died. Louisa didn't know what to do. She wanted to help, but she did not want to go home yet. As before, she turned to her writing. She wrote another novel, *Little Men*. She vowed to give all the money from the book to Anna and her two sons. *Little Men* also was a hit.

Louisa was uncomfortable with her new fame. Sometimes people asked for her autograph. She did not like that. She liked to stay in the background. She still believed strongly in helping others, especially other people who had less. She devoted much of her time to helping needy children. She continued to watch over her family. Yet she couldn't do everything.

When Louisa was forty-four, she and Abba became ill. Their family thought the two might die. Louisa kept on writing in spite of her illness. She wrote another children's book, *Under the Lilacs*. A few months later, Abba died in Louisa's arms.

Abba's death was hard on Louisa. "My only comfort is that I could make her last years comfortable," Louisa said. She wrote a poem about her mother after Abba's death.

Shortly after Abba died the family received some good news. May was getting married! Louisa sent them $1,000 as a wedding gift.

THE FINAL CHAPTER

Louisa no longer had the energy to write novels. Instead, she wrote short stories for children. She also watched her father with pride. Bronson finally had found his place. He was dean of a new school of philosophy in Boston. Louisa was happy for her father. Yet she wished the philosophers would change. She felt they should do things to help poor people instead of talk about them.

She preferred righting wrongs. At the time, women could not vote. Louisa worked to change that law. She got other women to work for it, too. Eventually, they succeeded. Louisa was the first registered female voter in Concord.

Her excitement over that victory did not last long. Her sister May died later that year. In her will, May asked Louisa to care for her daughter. May had named her daughter Louisa May, too. Little Louisa, or Lulu, came to live with Louisa. Now, she had to write, care for her family and care for Lulu. She combined some of her duties. She wrote a volume of stories for Lulu.

She also prepared for her death. She destroyed her mother's journal. She burned some of her letters. She wanted to keep parts of her life private. She knew she did not have long to live. She did not know that, in 1888, she would die just two days after her father. Bronson was 88. Louisa was 55.

Louisa May Alcott believed in the equality of all people, especially women. These women are demonstrating for voting rights.

The Alcott family held a joint funeral for Bronson and Louisa. The minister said, "So this daughter, such a support to her father on Earth, was needed by him even in heaven."

Before she died, Louisa adopted one of Anna's sons. He became her legal heir. Her heirs have watched over her manuscripts ever since. In 1994, a collector sold one of her manuscripts to a publisher for $1 million. The manuscript's title is *A Long Fatal Love Chase*.

Louisa had given that manuscript to her publisher in 1866. He rejected it. He said it was too "long and too sensational." The book is a romantic thriller. It's about a young woman who travels through Europe.

Fans of Louisa May Alcott know *A Long Fatal Chase* must also be based in part on her life. Yet no one will ever know what parts are truth and what are fiction.

Louisa May Alcott.

GLOSSARY OF TERMS

Civil War — a conflict in American history between the Northern and Southern states over slavery.

Commune — a place where all residents own and share everything.

Mercury — a heavy silver-white liquid that is a metallic chemical element.

Paralyzed — to have lost the ability to move.

Slavery — when people are treated as property and forced to work without pay.

Thriller — an exciting novel or story.